I0415892

March 2012

INFORMATION SECURITY

IRS Needs to Further Enhance Internal Control over Financial Reporting and Taxpayer Data

GAO

Accountability ★ Integrity ★ Reliability

GAO

Accountability * Integrity * Reliability

Highlights

Highlights of GAO-12-393, a report to the Commissioner of Internal Revenue

INFORMATION SECURITY

IRS Needs to Further Enhance Internal Control over Financial Reporting and Taxpayer Data

Why GAO Did This Study

The Internal Revenue Service (IRS) has a demanding responsibility in collecting taxes, processing tax returns, and enforcing the nation's tax laws. It relies extensively on computerized systems to support its financial and mission-related operations and on information security controls to protect financial and sensitive taxpayer information that resides on those systems.

As part of its audit of IRS's fiscal years 2011 and 2010 financial statements, GAO assessed whether controls over key financial and tax-processing systems are effective in ensuring the confidentiality, integrity, and availability of financial and sensitive taxpayer information. To do this, GAO examined IRS information security policies, plans, and procedures; tested controls over key financial applications; and interviewed key agency officials at seven sites.

What GAO Recommends

GAO recommends that IRS take 6 actions to fully implement key components of its comprehensive information security program. In a separate report with limited distribution, GAO is recommending that IRS take 23 specific actions to correct newly identified control weaknesses. In commenting on a draft of this report, IRS agreed to develop a detailed corrective action plan to address each recommendation.

View GAO-12-393. For more information, contact Nancy R. Kingsbury at (202) 512-2700 or kingsburyn@gao.gov or Gregory C. Wilshusen at (202) 512-6244 or wilshuseng@gao.gov.

What GAO Found

IRS implemented numerous controls and procedures intended to protect key financial and tax-processing systems; nevertheless, control weaknesses in these systems continue to jeopardize the confidentiality, integrity, and availability of the financial and sensitive taxpayer information processed by IRS's systems. Specifically, the agency continues to face challenges in controlling access to its information resources. For example, it had not always (1) implemented controls for identifying and authenticating users, such as requiring users to set new passwords after a prescribed period of time; (2) appropriately restricted access to certain servers; (3) ensured that sensitive data were encrypted when transmitted; (4) audited and monitored systems to ensure that unauthorized activities would be detected; or (5) ensured management validation of access to restricted areas. In addition, unpatched and outdated software exposed IRS to known vulnerabilities, and the agency had not enforced backup procedures for a key system.

An underlying reason for these weaknesses is that IRS has not fully implemented a comprehensive information security program. IRS has established a comprehensive framework for such a program, and has made strides to address control deficiencies—such as establishing working groups to identify and remediate specific at-risk control areas; however, it has not fully implemented all key components of its program. For example, IRS's security testing and monitoring continued to not detect many of the vulnerabilities GAO identified during this audit. IRS also did not promptly correct known vulnerabilities. For example, the agency indicated that 76 of the 105 previously reported weaknesses open at the end of GAO's prior year audit had not yet been corrected. In addition, IRS did not always validate that its actions to resolve known weaknesses were effectively implemented. Although IRS had a process in place for verifying whether each weakness had been corrected, this process was not always working as intended. Of the 29 weaknesses IRS indicated were corrected, GAO determined that 13 (about 45 percent) had not yet been fully addressed.

Considered collectively, these deficiencies, both new and unresolved from previous GAO audits, along with a lack of fully effective compensating and mitigating controls, impair IRS's ability to ensure that its financial and taxpayer information is secure from internal threats. This reduces IRS's assurance that its financial statements and other financial information are fairly presented or reliable and that sensitive IRS and taxpayer information is being sufficiently safeguarded from unauthorized disclosure or modification. These deficiencies are the basis of GAO's determination that IRS had a material weakness in internal control over financial reporting related to information security in fiscal year 2011.

_____ United States Government Accountability Office

Contents

Abbreviations

eCM	enterprise continuous monitoring
ESAT	Enterprise Security Audit Trails
FISMA	Federal Information Security Management Act
ID	identification
IRS	Internal Revenue Service
NIST	National Institute of Standards and Technology
OMB	Office of Management and Budget
SA&A	security assessment and authorization
TIGTA	Treasury Inspector General for Tax Administration

United States Government Accountability Office
Washington, DC 20548

March 16, 2012

The Honorable Douglas H. Shulman
Commissioner of Internal Revenue

Dear Commissioner Shulman:

The Internal Revenue Service (IRS) has a demanding responsibility in collecting taxes, processing tax returns, and enforcing the nation's tax laws. It relies extensively on computerized systems to support its financial and mission-related operations and on information security controls to protect the confidentiality, integrity, and availability of the financial and sensitive taxpayer information that resides on those systems.[1]

As part of our audit of IRS's fiscal years 2011 and 2010 financial statements, we assessed the effectiveness of the agency's information security controls over its key financial and tax-processing systems, information, and interconnected networks at seven locations.[2] These systems support the processing, storage, and transmission of financial and sensitive taxpayer information. In our report on IRS's fiscal years 2011 and 2010 financial statements, we reported that IRS continued to

---

[1]Information security controls include logical and physical access controls, configuration management, segregation of duties, and continuity of operations. These controls are designed to ensure that access to data is appropriately restricted, physical access to sensitive computing resources and facilities is protected, systems are securely configured to avoid exposure to known vulnerabilities, incompatible duties are segregated among individuals, and backup and recovery plans are adequate and tested to ensure the continuity of essential operations.

[2]GAO, *Financial Audit: IRS's Fiscal Years 2011 and 2010 Financial Statements,* GAO-12-165 (Washington, D.C.: Nov. 10, 2011).

have a material weakness in internal control over financial reporting related to information security in fiscal year 2011.[3]

Our objective was to determine whether IRS's controls over key financial and tax-processing systems are effective in ensuring the confidentiality, integrity, and availability of financial and sensitive taxpayer information. To do this, we examined IRS information security policies, plans, and procedures; tested controls over key financial applications; interviewed key agency officials; and reviewed our prior reports to identify previously reported weaknesses and assessed the effectiveness of corrective actions taken. We concentrated our evaluation on threats emanating from sources internal to IRS's computer networks.

We performed our audit from April 2011 to March 2012 in accordance with U.S. generally accepted government auditing standards. We believe our audit provides a reasonable basis for our opinions and other conclusions. For additional information about our objective, scope, and methodology, refer to appendix I.

Background

The use of information technology has created many benefits for agencies such as IRS in achieving their missions and providing information and services to the public, but extensive reliance on computerized information also creates challenges in securing that information from various threats. Information security is especially important for government agencies, where maintaining the public's trust is essential.

Without proper safeguards, computer systems are vulnerable to individuals and groups with malicious intentions who can intrude and use their access to obtain sensitive information, commit fraud, disrupt operations, or launch attacks against other computer systems and

---

[3]A material weakness is a deficiency, or a combination of deficiencies, in internal control such that there is a reasonable possibility that a material misstatement of the entity's financial statements will not be prevented, or detected and corrected, on a timely basis. A deficiency in internal control exists when the design or operation of a control does not allow management or employees, in the normal course of performing their assigned functions, to prevent, or detect and correct, misstatements on a timely basis. Materiality represents the magnitude of an omission or misstatement of an item in a financial report that, when considered in light of surrounding circumstances, makes it probable that the judgment of a reasonable person relying on the information would have been changed or influenced by the inclusion or correction of the item.

networks. Concerns about the risk to these systems are well founded for a number of reasons, including the increase in reports of security incidents, the ease of obtaining and using hacking tools, and steady advances in the sophistication and effectiveness of attack technology. The Federal Bureau of Investigation has identified multiple sources of threats, including foreign entities engaged in intelligence gathering and information warfare, domestic criminals, hackers, virus writers, and disgruntled employees or contractors working within an organization. In addition, the U.S. Secret Service and the CERT® Coordination Center[4] studied insider threats in the government sector and stated in a January 2008 report that "government sector insiders have the potential to pose a substantial threat by virtue of their knowledge of, and access to, employer systems and/or databases."[5] Insider threats include errors or mistakes and fraudulent or malevolent acts by insiders.

Our previous reports, and those by federal inspectors general, describe persistent information security weaknesses that place federal agencies, including IRS, at risk of disruption, fraud, or inappropriate disclosure of sensitive information. Accordingly, we have designated information security as a governmentwide high-risk area since 1997, most recently in 2011.[6]

Information security is essential to creating and maintaining effective internal controls. The Federal Managers' Financial Integrity Act of 1982 requires us to prescribe standards for internal control in federal agencies.[7] The standards provide the overall framework for establishing and maintaining internal control and for identifying and addressing major performance and management challenges and areas at greatest risk of fraud, waste, abuse, and mismanagement.[8] The term "internal control" is

---

[4]The CERT® Coordination Center is a center of Internet security expertise located at the Software Engineering Institute, a federally funded research and development center operated by Carnegie Mellon University.

[5]U.S. Secret Service and Computer Emergency Response Team, *Insider Threat Study: Illicit Cyber Activity in the Government Sector* (Washington, D.C., and Pittsburgh, Pa.: January 2008).

[6]GAO, *High-Risk Series: Information Management and Technology*, GAO/HR-97-9 (Washington, D.C.: February 1997), and *High-Risk Series: An Update*, GAO-11-278 (Washington, D.C.: February 2011).

[7]See 31 U.S.C. § 3511.

[8]GAO, *Standards for Internal Control in the Federal Government*, GAO/AIMD-00-21.3.1 (Washington, D.C.: November 1999).

synonymous with the term "management control," which covers all aspects of an agency's operations (programmatic, financial, and compliance). The attitude and philosophy of management toward information systems can have a profound effect on internal control. Information system controls consist of those internal controls that are dependent on information systems processing and include general controls (security management, access controls, configuration management, segregation of duties, and contingency planning) at the entitywide, system, and business process application levels; business process application controls (input, processing, output, master file, interface, and data management system controls); and user controls (controls performed by people interacting with information systems).

Recognizing the importance of securing federal agencies' information systems, Congress enacted the Federal Information Security Management Act (FISMA) in December 2002 to strengthen the security of information and systems within federal agencies.[9] FISMA requires each agency to develop, document, and implement an agencywide information security program for the information and information systems that support the operations and assets of the agency, using a risk-based approach to information security management. Such a program includes assessing risk; developing and implementing cost-effective security plans, policies, and procedures; providing specialized training; testing and evaluating the effectiveness of controls; planning, implementing, evaluating, and documenting remedial actions to address information security deficiencies; and ensuring continuity of operations. The act also assigned to the National Institute of Standards and Technology (NIST) the responsibility for developing standards and guidelines that include minimum information security requirements.

IRS Is the Tax Collector for the United States	IRS has demanding responsibilities in collecting taxes, processing tax returns, and enforcing federal tax laws, and relies extensively on computerized systems to support its financial and mission-related operations. In fiscal years 2011 and 2010, IRS collected about $2.4 trillion and $2.3 trillion, respectively, in federal tax payments; processed hundreds of millions of tax and information returns; and paid about $416

[9]FISMA was enacted as title III, E-Government Act of 2002, Pub L. No. 107-347, Dec. 17, 2002.

billion and $467 billion, respectively, in refunds to taxpayers. Further, the size and complexity of IRS add unique operational challenges. IRS employs over 100,000 people in its Washington, D.C., headquarters and over 700 offices in all 50 states and U.S. territories and in some U.S. embassies and consulates. To manage its data and information, the agency operates three enterprise computing centers located in Detroit, Michigan; Martinsburg, West Virginia; and Memphis, Tennessee. IRS also collects and maintains a significant amount of personal and financial information on each U.S. taxpayer. Protecting the confidentiality of this sensitive information is paramount; otherwise, taxpayers could be exposed to loss of privacy and to financial loss and damages resulting from identity theft or other financial crimes.

The Commissioner of Internal Revenue has overall responsibility for ensuring the confidentiality, integrity, and availability of the information and information systems that support the agency and its operations. FISMA requires the chief information officer or comparable official at a federal agency to be responsible for developing and maintaining an information security program. IRS has delegated this responsibility to the Associate Chief Information Officer for Cybersecurity, who heads the Office of Cybersecurity. The Office of Cybersecurity's mission is to protect taxpayer information and IRS's electronic systems, services, and data from internal and external cybersecurity-related threats by implementing security practices in planning, implementation, risk management, and operations. IRS develops and publishes its information security policies, guidelines, standards, and procedures in the *Internal Revenue Manual* and other documents in order for IRS divisions and offices to carry out their respective responsibilities in information security. In October 2011, the Treasury Inspector General for Tax Administration (TIGTA) stated that security of taxpayer data, including securing computer systems, was the top priority in its list of top 10 management challenges for IRS in fiscal year 2012.[10]

---

[10]TIGTA, *Management and Performance Challenges Facing the Internal Revenue Service for Fiscal Year 2012* (Washington, D.C.: October 2011).

IRS Has Made Progress, but Control Weaknesses Continue to Place Financial and Taxpayer Information at Risk

Despite IRS's efforts, weaknesses in controls over key financial and tax-processing systems continue to jeopardize the confidentiality, integrity, and availability of financial and taxpayer information. Specifically, IRS continues to face challenges in controlling access to its information resources. Although IRS has various initiatives under way to address control weaknesses, it has not consistently or fully implemented controls for identifying and authenticating users, authorizing access to resources, ensuring that sensitive data are encrypted, monitoring actions taken on its systems, or controlling physical access to its resources. In addition, outdated and unsupported software exposes IRS to known vulnerabilities, and shortcomings in performing system backup place the availability of data at risk. An underlying reason for these weaknesses is that IRS has not fully implemented key components of its information security program. These include completing corrective actions for identified weaknesses in its risk assessment process; establishing consistent and specific policies and procedures; ensuring that security plans reflect IRS's current environment; ensuring that contractors receive security training; effectively testing and evaluating policies, procedures, and controls; and validating corrective action plans. During fiscal year 2011, IRS management devoted attention and resources to addressing the agency's information security control weaknesses. However, until IRS takes further steps to correct these weaknesses, financial and taxpayer data are at increased risk of unauthorized disclosure, modification, or destruction, which could result in misstatement of financial data and management decisions that are based on unreliable information.

IRS Continues to Face Challenges in Controlling Access to Information Resources

A basic management objective for any organization is to protect the resources that support its critical operations from unauthorized access. Organizations accomplish this objective by designing and implementing controls that are intended to prevent, limit, and detect unauthorized access to computing resources, programs, information, and facilities. Access controls include those related to user identification and authentication, authorization, cryptography, audit and monitoring, and physical security. However, IRS did not fully implement effective controls in these areas. Without adequate access controls, unauthorized individuals may be able to log in, access sensitive information, and make undetected changes or deletions for malicious purposes or personal gain. In addition, authorized individuals may be able to intentionally or unintentionally view, add, modify, or delete data to which they should not have been given access.

Controls Were Not Consistently Implemented for Identifying and Authenticating Users

A computer system needs to be able to identify and authenticate each user so that activities on the system can be linked and traced to a specific individual. An organization does this by assigning a unique user account to each user, and in so doing, the system is able to distinguish one user from another—a process called identification (ID). The system also needs to establish the validity of a user's claimed identity by requesting some kind of information, such as a password, that is known only by the user—a process known as authentication. The combination of identification and authentication—such as user account-password combinations—provides the basis for establishing individual accountability and for controlling access to the system. The *Internal Revenue Manual* requires the use of a strong password for authentication (defined as a minimum of eight characters, containing at least one numeric or special character, and a mixture of at least one uppercase and one lowercase letter). The manual also states that database account passwords are not to be reused within 10 password changes and that the password grace period for a database—the number of days an individual has to change his or her password after it expires—should be set to 10.

IRS had implemented various password controls, but weaknesses existed. For the Oracle database supporting its authorization system, IRS enforced strong password policies on active user accounts. However, IRS did not set appropriate password reuse maximum time or ensure complex password verification checking for its procurement system. As a result of these weaknesses, increased risk exists that an individual with malicious intentions could gain inappropriate access to sensitive IRS applications and data on these systems, and potentially use the access to attempt compromises of other IRS systems.

Weaknesses in Authorization Controls Limited Their Effectiveness

Authorization is the process of granting or denying access rights and permissions to a protected resource, such as a network, a system, an application, a function, or a file. According to NIST, access control policies and access enforcement mechanisms are employed by organizations to control access between users (or processes acting on behalf of users) and objects in the information system. Furthermore, it notes that access enforcement mechanisms are employed at the application level, when necessary, to provide increased information security for the organization. According to the *Internal Revenue Manual*, the agency should implement access control measures that provide protection from unauthorized alteration, loss, unavailability, or disclosure of information. The manual also requires that system access should be granted based on the principle of least privilege—allowing access at the minimum level necessary to support a user's job duties. In addition, its policy states that a servicewide medium/process shall be used to register all users for access to any IRS information technology resource to which they require access. IRS policy also requires that all accounts be deactivated within 1 week of an individual's departure on friendly terms and immediately on an individual's departure on unfriendly terms.

IRS has taken steps to address access authorization controls, but weaknesses exist. For example, it has appropriately restricted access to disaster recovery servers, and has implemented a capability to identify and correct potential anomalies in mainframe access definitions. Also, it has removed users with inappropriate access to a mainframe database supporting a financial system. However, additional authorization controls were not always functioning as intended, and access authorization policies were not effectively implemented. For example, systems used to process tax and financial information did not fully prevent access by unauthorized users or excessive levels of access for authorized users. More specifically, IRS has implemented an access authorization control for a system used to process electronic tax payment information; however, users had the capability to circumvent this control and gain access to this system's server. Insecurely configured software used to support this system also exposed it to unauthorized users. In addition, IRS's compliance checks revealed unauthorized access to another system. During its monthly compliance check in August 2011, the agency identified 16 users who had been granted access to the procurement system without receiving approval from the agency's authorization system. Also, the data in a shared work area used to support accounting operations were fully accessible by network administration staff although they did not need such access. Further, IRS has not taken actions to appropriately restrict services and user access, and to remove active application accounts in a timely manner for employees who had separated or no longer needed access.

IRS noted additional authorization controls to compensate for or mitigate known deficiencies; however, these controls were not always implemented. For example, although IRS cited the use of role-based access for a major system used to process taxpayer data, this control was not yet implemented. Until IRS appropriately controls users' access to its systems and effectively implements its procedures for authorization, the agency has limited assurance that its information resources are protected from unauthorized access, alteration, and disclosure.

Certain Sensitive Data Are Transmitted across the IRS Network Unencrypted	Cryptography underlies many of the mechanisms used to enforce the confidentiality and integrity of critical and sensitive information. A basic element of cryptography is encryption, which is used to transform plain text into cipher text using a special value known as a key and a mathematical process known as an algorithm. According to IRS policy, the use of insecure protocols should be restricted because their widespread use can allow passwords and other sensitive data to be transmitted across its internal network unencrypted.

IRS continued to expand its use of encryption to protect sensitive data, but shortcomings remain. IRS took action to encrypt data transfers for its administrative accounting system. However, as we reported in 2011, the agency configured a server that transfers tax and financial data between internal systems to use protocols that allowed unencrypted transmission of sensitive data.[11] IRS also had not rectified its use of unencrypted protocols for a sensitive tax-processing application, potentially exposing user ID and password combinations. By not encrypting sensitive data, increased risk exists that an unauthorized individual could view and then use the data to gain unwarranted access to its system or sensitive information.

Although Audit and Monitoring Processes Were in Place, They Were Not Always Effective	To establish individual accountability, monitor compliance with security policies, and investigate security violations, it is crucial to determine what, when, and by whom specific actions have been taken on a system. Organizations accomplish this by implementing system or security software that provides an audit trail—a log of system activity—that they can use to determine the source of a transaction or attempted transaction and to monitor users' activities. The way in which organizations configure system or security software determines the nature and extent of information that can be provided by the audit trail. To be effective, organizations should configure their software to collect and maintain audit trails that are sufficient to track security-relevant events. The *Internal Revenue Manual* requires systems to implement operational and technical control guidance to monitor traffic on host intrusion detection systems, and also states that IRS should enable and configure audit logging on all systems to aid in the detection of security violations, performance problems, and flaws in applications. Additionally, IRS policy

---

[11] GAO, *Information Security: IRS Needs to Enhance Control over Financial Reporting and Taxpayer Data*, GAO-11-308 (Washington, D.C.: Mar. 15, 2011).

states that security controls in information systems shall be monitored on an ongoing basis.

IRS had established several activities designed to support detection of questionable or unauthorized access to financial applications and data and to support its response; however, some of these activities were not fully in place or operating as intended. To assist in its audit and monitoring activities, IRS established the Enterprise Security Audit Trails (ESAT) Project Management Office, which is responsible for managing all enterprise audit initiatives and identifying and overseeing deployment and transition of various audit trail solutions. The program is currently in its early stages, but the agency is continually implementing new procedures building on the program's initiatives. For fiscal year 2011, the agency had ESAT-related audit processes in place for four systems—only one of which was relevant to our financial statement audit efforts. However, the processes were not yet operating effectively. For example, ESAT had not delivered system audit reports covering a 4-month period for one financial application to the Office of the Chief Financial Officer in a timely manner, and appropriate management officials were not aware of this shortcoming.

Other monitoring activities were also not always operating effectively. Although IRS had enabled audit logging for certain systems, it had not for others. For example, the agency had enabled and configured audit logging for UNIX operating systems on 31 servers reviewed. However, it had not enabled and configured monitoring activity for its authorization system. IRS officials recognized this shortcoming and indicated that they are working with cybersecurity staff to resolve this deficiency. Finally, IRS did not properly enable auditing features on its Oracle databases supporting three systems we reviewed. As a result of detection and response capabilities not being fully in place and certain deficiencies in configurations, IRS's ability to establish individual accountability, monitor compliance with security policies, and investigate security violations was limited.

Physical Access Control Procedures Were Not Consistently Implemented

Physical security controls are important for protecting computer facilities and resources from espionage, sabotage, damage, and theft. These controls involve procedures to authorize employees' access to and control over unissued keys or other entry devices. At IRS, physical access control measures, such as physical access cards that are used to permit or deny access to certain areas of a facility, are vital to safeguarding its facilities, computing resources, and information from internal and external threats. The *Internal Revenue Manual* requires access controls that safeguard assets against possible theft and malicious actions. IRS policy also requires completion of appropriate access authorization documentation prior to issuance of physical access cards, and that such entry devices be inventoried once every 24 hours of each workday, including signing the inventory to verify that it has been completed.

IRS implemented numerous physical security controls at its enterprise computing centers to safeguard assets against possible theft and malicious actions. For example, IRS had a dedicated guard force at each of its computing centers to, among other things, control physical access to restricted areas and secure entry devices such as physical access cards. In addition, the 30 individuals we selected for review had appropriate access to secure computing areas at the computing centers, and IRS had appropriately restricted access to master keys at the centers that used them. Further, IRS effectively screened visitors, and at one computing center, reviewed lists of employees authorized to enter restricted areas.

Nevertheless, IRS did not always consistently authorize employees' access to restricted areas or inventory physical access cards. At each of the computing centers, IRS had a process in place to authorize employees' access to restricted areas. However, one of the centers did not document this authorization for 7 of 20 employees whose access authority we reviewed. In addition, although the guard force at each computing center performed an inventory to account for physical access cards, they did not consistently implement this control. For example, the guard forces at two of the three computing centers we visited did not always sign, thus providing accountability for, the inventory of physical access cards. In addition, at least one of three guard shifts did not detect an anomaly in the inventory for 4 of the 5 days we reviewed at one computing center. Further, several physical security weaknesses identified during previous audits remain unresolved. These include issues concerning management validation of access to restricted areas, proximity cards allowing inappropriate access, and unlocked cabinets containing network devices. As a result, IRS has reduced assurance that its computing resources and sensitive information are adequately protected from unauthorized access. In addition, IRS has cited its physical security controls as compensating or mitigating controls for other noted deficiencies; however, because of the weaknesses noted in these controls, IRS may not be able to rely on physical security as a compensating control.

Weaknesses in Other Information Security Controls Introduce Risk

In addition to access controls, other important controls should be in place to ensure the confidentiality, integrity, and availability of an organization's information. These controls include policies, procedures, and techniques for securely configuring information systems; segregating incompatible duties; and planning for continuity of operations.

Systems Were Not Securely Configured, Exposing IRS to Known Vulnerabilities

Configuration management involves, among other things, (1) verifying the correctness of the security settings in the operating systems, applications, or computing and network devices and (2) obtaining reasonable assurance that systems are configured and operating securely and as intended. Patch management, a component of configuration management, is an important element in mitigating the risks associated with software vulnerabilities. When a software vulnerability is discovered, the software vendor may develop and distribute a patch or work-around to mitigate the vulnerability. Without the patch, an attacker can exploit a software vulnerability to read, modify, or delete sensitive information; disrupt operations; or launch attacks against systems at another organization. Outdated and unsupported software is more vulnerable to attack and exploitation because vendors no longer provide updates, including security updates. Accordingly, the *Internal Revenue Manual* states that IRS will manage systems to reduce vulnerabilities by promptly installing patches. Specifically, it states that security patches should be applied within 30 days, and hardware and software on network devices should be promptly maintained and updated in response to identified vulnerabilities. The manual also states that system administrators should ensure the version of the operating system being used is one for which the vendor still offers standardized technical support.

IRS made progress in updating certain systems. For example, the agency had provided an effective patch management solution for its Windows servers. IRS also upgraded its domain name system servers at the three computing centers.

However, the agency did not always apply critical patches or ensure that versions of its operating systems were still supported by the vendor. For example, for one system we reviewed, the agency had not applied a security-related patch release within 30 days of its issuance to the UNIX operating system for 10 of the 14 production servers reviewed; the vendor issued the patch release in April 2011, but IRS had not yet installed it at the time of our site visit in June 2011.[12] In addition, IRS had never installed numerous patch releases for the UNIX operating system supporting another system we reviewed, although this operating system has existed since March 2009. The 10 uninstalled security-related patch releases were considered "critical" by the vendor. By not installing security patches in a timely fashion, IRS increases the risk that known vulnerabilities in its systems may be exploited. The agency also used outdated software on all three reviewed servers used for remote access. Further, as we reported in March 2011, IRS was using unsupported versions of software on most network devices reviewed.[13] Running outdated and unsupported operating systems increases security exposure, as the vendor will not be supplying any security patches to the unsupported operating system.

IRS Appropriately Segregated Incompatible Duties

Segregation of duties refers to the policies, procedures, and organizational structures that help ensure that no single individual can independently control all key aspects of a process or computer-related operation and thereby gain unauthorized access to assets or records. Often, organizations achieve segregation of duties by dividing responsibilities among two or more individuals or organizational groups. This diminishes the likelihood that errors and wrongful acts will go undetected, because the activities of one individual or group will serve as a check on the activities of the other. Conversely, inadequate segregation of duties increases the risk that erroneous or fraudulent transactions could be processed, improper program changes implemented, and computer resources damaged or destroyed. The *Internal Revenue Manual* requires that IRS divide and separate duties and responsibilities of functions among different individuals so that no individual has all necessary authority and system access to disrupt or corrupt a critical security process. In addition, IRS policy states that the primary security role of any database administrator is to administer and maintain database repositories for proper use by authorized individuals and that database administrators should not have system administrator access rights.

IRS implemented appropriate segregation of duties controls. Specifically, IRS implemented controls to prevent the assignment of incompatible database and system access privileges that allow for the compromise of

---

[12]A patch release can contain multiple patches for a system.

[13]GAO-11-308.

separation-of-duties controls. The agency also segregated duties for database and system administration for its procurement system. As a result, IRS has increased assurance that errors or wrongful acts will be detected.

IRS Has Contingency Plans in Place, but Details for a System's Plan Are Lacking, and Backup Procedures Were Not Always Effectively Implemented

According to NIST, contingency planning is a critical component of emergency management and organizational resilience. To ensure that mission-critical operations continue, organizations should be able to detect, mitigate, and recover from service disruptions while preserving access to vital information. One facet of ensuring that mission-critical operations can be recovered is establishing an information system recovery and reconstitution capability so that the information system can be restored to its original state after a service disruption. Conducting a business impact analysis is a key step in the contingency planning process. A business impact analysis is an analysis of information technology system requirements, processes, and interdependencies used to characterize system contingency requirements and priorities in the event of a significant disruption. Moreover, it correlates the system with the critical mission/business processes and services provided, and based on that information, characterizes the consequences of a disruption. In addition, developing an information system contingency plan is a critical step in the process of implementing a comprehensive contingency planning program. Organizations should prepare plans that are clearly documented, communicated to staff who could be affected, and updated to reflect current operations. Further, testing contingency plans is essential in determining whether the plans will function as intended in an emergency situation. Another key aspect of contingency planning is the development of a disaster recovery plan. A disaster recovery plan is an information system-focused plan designed to restore operability of the target system, application, or computer facility infrastructure at an alternate site after an emergency. The information system contingency plan differs from a disaster recovery plan primarily in that the information system contingency plan procedures are developed for recovery of the system regardless of site or location. In contrast, a disaster recovery plan is primarily a site-specific plan.

The *Internal Revenue Manual* requires business impact analyses for systems, and includes steps for completing this process. More specifically, the business impact analysis should (1) identify business requirements and the purpose of the application undergoing the business impact analysis, (2) identify outage tolerances and impacts, and (3) identify recovery priorities. The manual also requires that IRS develop, test, and maintain information system contingency plans for all systems, and review and update these plans. In addition, IRS policy calls for the development of disaster recovery plans for each information system to ensure that, after disruption, the system can be restored to its full operational status. Moreover, the policy notes that the disaster recovery plan should define the resources, roles, responsibilities, actions, tasks, and the detailed work steps (keystrokes) required to restore an information technology system to its full operational status at the current or alternate facility after a major disruption with long-term effects. Further, according to policy, IRS shall implement and enforce backup procedures for all systems and information.

IRS had processes in place to ensure continuity of operations; however, one of the disaster recovery plans we reviewed lacked detail, and backup procedures were not always effectively implemented for a key tax-processing system.

- For the five business impact analyses that we reviewed, IRS generally developed these business impact analyses by identifying business requirements and the purpose of the application, outage tolerances and impacts, and recovery priorities.

- IRS had developed, reviewed, and updated the five information system contingency plans that we reviewed. Further, these plans were tested within the past year.

- For the five disaster recovery plans that we reviewed, IRS had generally developed these plans defining the resources, roles, and responsibilities required to restore the respective systems to their full operational status. However, the disaster recovery plan for IRS's system used to authorize access to its information resources did not include detailed work steps (keystrokes) required to restore the system.

- IRS did not effectively implement and enforce backup procedures for a key tax-processing system. As a result, during a fiscal year 2011 test, IRS was unable to demonstrate continuity of business processes for a key system used to process taxpayer data. Specifically, although agency officials noted that the operating system component was able to be restored, the system was missing 1 week of critical data essential for business processing because the backup process was not executed as planned. With the exception of this system, all other systems reviewed, which had conducted a disaster recovery test, demonstrated that they were able to be successfully recovered.

Until the agency develops a disaster recovery plan for its authorization system to include detailed work steps (keystrokes) required to restore the system, and effectively implements and enforces its backup procedures for its system used to process taxpayer data, IRS may be unable to restore its authorization system to its full operational status after a major disruption, and its ability to reconstitute key business processes critical to IRS's mission may be limited.

IRS Has Not Fully Implemented Key Components of Its Information Security Program

A key reason for the information security weaknesses in IRS's financial and tax-processing systems is that it has not yet fully implemented critical components of its comprehensive information security program. FISMA requires each agency to develop, document, and implement an information security program that, among other things, includes

- periodic assessments of the risk and magnitude of harm that could result from the unauthorized access, use, disclosure, disruption, modification, or destruction of information and information systems;

- policies and procedures that (1) are based on risk assessments, (2) cost-effectively reduce information security risks to an acceptable level, (3) ensure that information security is addressed throughout the life cycle of each system, and (4) ensure compliance with applicable requirements;

- plans for providing adequate information security for networks, facilities, and systems;

- security awareness training to inform personnel of information security risks and of their responsibilities in complying with agency policies and procedures, as well as training personnel with significant security responsibilities for information security;

- periodic testing and evaluation of the effectiveness of information security policies, procedures, and practices, to be performed with a frequency depending on risk, but no less than annually, and that includes testing of management, operational, and technical controls for every system identified in the agency's required inventory of major information systems; and

- a process for planning, implementing, evaluating, and documenting remedial action to address any deficiencies in its information security policies, procedures, or practices.

IRS has made progress in developing and documenting certain elements of its information security program. During fiscal year 2011, IRS management devoted attention and resources to addressing the agency's information security controls. For example, IRS formed cross-functional working groups with knowledge of its internal systems to address identified areas considered at risk. IRS also acknowledged that maintaining effective information security controls, at the individual system or component level in its large internal network, presents significant challenges. In addition, the agency cited actions taken to implement additional controls designed to partially compensate for and mitigate the risks associated with previously identified information security weaknesses, including weaknesses related to its internal network, database, and mainframe security; procurement and administrative accounting applications; and internal control monitoring. However, as we reported in our fiscal year 2011 financial audit report, these additional controls were not always operating as intended or were not effective in compensating for the associated weaknesses.[14]

To bolster the security of its networks and systems and to address its information security weaknesses, IRS has provided a comprehensive framework for its information security program. The agency has initiatives under way to further enhance its security posture. For example, during fiscal year 2011, IRS continued to implement a Security Compliance and Posture Monitoring and Reporting program to measure, monitor, and report compliance with security controls. As long as these efforts remain flexible to address changing technology and evolving threats, include our findings and those of TIGTA in measuring success, and are fully and effectively implemented, they should improve the agency's overall information security posture.

However, despite establishing a comprehensive framework for its information security program, IRS has not fully implemented all components of its program. These include identifying risks; ensuring consistent and specific policies and procedures; updating all system security plans; providing security training to all personnel, including contractors; effectively testing and evaluating policies, procedures, and controls; and validating corrective actions.

---

[14]GAO-12-165.

Although IRS Generally Prepared Risk Assessments, It Had Not Yet Completed One for a Key System

According to NIST, risk is determined by identifying potential threats to the organization and vulnerabilities in its systems, determining the likelihood that a particular threat may exploit vulnerabilities, and assessing the resulting impact on the organization's mission, including the effect on sensitive and critical systems and data. Identifying and assessing information security risks are essential to determining what controls are required. Moreover, by increasing awareness of risks, these assessments can generate support for the policies and controls that are adopted in order to help ensure that these policies and controls operate as intended. In conjunction with NIST guidance, IRS requires its risk assessment process to detail the residual risk assessed, as well as potential threats, and to recommend corrective actions for reducing or eliminating the vulnerabilities identified.[15] The *Internal Revenue Manual* also requires system risk assessments to be reviewed annually and updated a minimum of every 3 years or whenever there is a significant change to the system, the facilities where the system resides, or other conditions that may affect the security or status of system accreditation.

IRS had processes in place to identify and assess information security risks for the five systems that we reviewed. For example, the agency used a detailed methodology to conduct risk assessments with key steps that include threat and vulnerability identification, control analysis, impact analysis, and mitigation recommendations. The risk assessments that we reviewed included, among other things, risk and severity level determination, impact analyses, and recommendations to correct or mitigate threats and vulnerabilities that were identified. Further, IRS also addressed a previously identified weakness regarding ensuring the review of risk assessments for its systems on at least an annual basis.

Although IRS had a risk assessment process in place, it had not fully implemented the process. For example, IRS's general ledger system for tax-related activities was moved from one mainframe environment to another at a different facility, but the risk assessment was not updated. We previously recommended that IRS update the assessment, and the agency was in the process of addressing this issue at the time of our review. Until IRS fully implements its policies and procedures for risk assessments, potential risks to its systems and the adequacy of associated security controls to reduce these risks could be unknown.

---

[15]Residual risk is the risk remaining after the implementation of new or enhanced controls.

IRS Generally Documented Its Information Security Policies and Procedures, but Some Had Not Been Fully Developed or Documented

Another key element of an effective information security program is to develop, document, and implement risk-based policies, procedures, and technical standards that govern the security of an agency's computing environment. If properly developed and implemented, policies and procedures should help reduce the risk associated with unauthorized access or disruption of services. Technical security standards can provide consistent implementation guidance for each computing environment. Developing, documenting, and implementing security policies are the primary mechanisms by which management communicates its views and requirements; these policies also serve as the basis for adopting specific procedures and technical controls. In addition, agencies need to take the actions necessary to effectively implement or execute these procedures and controls. Otherwise, agency systems and information will not receive the protection that the security policies and controls should provide.

With only a few exceptions, IRS had developed and documented its information security policies and procedures. These policies and procedures generally address multiple information security components, including risk assessment, security planning, security training, testing and evaluating security controls, and contingency planning. However, we noted instances where documentation had not been fully developed or documented for systems that we reviewed. For example, IRS had not

- documented a baseline configuration standard for tasks initiated on its mainframe operating system;

- documented monitoring procedures that staff used to review audit logs for a key financial system;

- fully documented monitoring procedures for its procurement system, specifically supervisory review procedures for ensuring access privileges were appropriate for segregation of duties; or

- addressed prior recommendations associated with policies and procedures. These recommendations covered issues such as securely configuring routers to encrypt network traffic, configuring switches to defend against attacks that could crash the network, notifying the Computer Security Incident Response Center of network changes that could affect its ability to detect unauthorized access, and ensuring password controls are consistent.

Without comprehensive and fully documented policies and procedures, IRS has limited assurance that staff will consistently implement effective controls over systems and that its information systems will be protected as intended. For example, we identified shortcomings in controls associated with the mainframe configuration and system monitoring.

IRS Documented Management, Operational, and Technical Controls in Security Plans, but One Plan Did Not Reflect the Current Environment

An objective of system security planning is to improve the protection of information technology resources. A system security plan provides an overview of the system's security requirements and describes the controls that are in place or planned to meet those requirements. The Office of Management and Budget's (OMB) Circular A-130 requires that agencies develop system security plans for major applications and general support systems, and that these plans address policies and procedures for providing management, operational, and technical controls. In addition, the *Internal Revenue Manual* requires that security plans for information systems be developed, documented, implemented, reviewed annually, and updated a minimum of every 3 years or whenever there is a significant change to the system. In addition, these plans should describe the security controls in place or planned for IRS systems.

IRS generally had developed, documented, and updated its system security plans. IRS documented its management, operational, and technical controls in each of the five security plans that we reviewed. These plans were also reviewed within the 3-year time period as required by IRS policy and included information as required by OMB Circular A-130 for major applications and general support systems. However, in March 2011, we reported that the system security plan for one application still reflected controls from the previous environment even though IRS had moved this application from one mainframe to another. We recommended that IRS update the application security plan to describe controls in place in its current mainframe operating environment. IRS had initiated, but not completed, its efforts to update the plan. Without an updated system security plan for this major financial application, IRS cannot ensure that the most appropriate security controls are in place to protect the critical information this system houses.

IRS Ensured Its Employees, but Not Its Contractors, Received Security Awareness and Specialized Training

People are one of the weakest links in attempts to secure systems and networks. Therefore, an important component of an information security program is providing sufficient training so that users understand system security risks and their own role in implementing related policies and controls to mitigate those risks. The *Internal Revenue Manual* requires that all personnel performing information technology security duties meet minimum continuing professional education hours in accordance with their roles. Individuals performing a security role are required by IRS to have 12, 8, or 4 hours of specialized training per year, depending on their specific role. IRS policy also requires that all new employees and contractors receive security awareness training within the first 10 working days.

IRS had processes in place for providing employees with security awareness and specialized training. All employees with specific security-related roles and newly hired employees that we reviewed met or exceeded the required minimum security awareness and specialized training hours. However, IRS did not always ensure that contractors received security awareness training. In March 2010, we reported that contractors had not received security awareness training within the first 10 working days and recommended that IRS address this weakness.[16] Nevertheless, IRS indicated that it had not yet implemented this recommendation. As a result, IRS has reduced assurance that its contractors are aware of information security risks associated with their roles and responsibilities.

Tests and Evaluations of Policies, Procedures, and Controls Were Not Always Effective

Another key element of an information security program is conducting tests and evaluations of policies, procedures, and controls to determine whether they are effective and operating as intended. This type of oversight is a fundamental element because it demonstrates management's commitment to the security program, reminds employees of their roles and responsibilities, and identifies areas of noncompliance and ineffectiveness. Although tests and evaluations of policies, procedures, and controls may encourage compliance with security policies, the full benefits are not achieved unless the results improve the security program through implementation of compensating or mitigating controls if needed. Consistent with FISMA, the *Internal Revenue Manual* states that annual security assessments will be conducted to determine if security controls are operating effectively and correctly implemented. In addition, the manual states that all IRS systems will be verified for configuration management compliance by using an approved compliance verification application.

---

[16]GAO, *IRS Needs to Continue to Address Significant Weaknesses,* GAO-10-355 (Washington, D.C.: Mar. 19, 2010).

IRS has processes in place for performing tests and evaluations of policies, procedures, and controls. As part of its test and evaluations process, the agency uses NIST Special Publication 800-53A to select controls that are applicable to each system. To comply with IRS policy, all selected system controls were tested during the security assessment and authorization (SA&A) process, which occurs every 3 years or whenever there is a significant change to the system. Between authorization assessments, IRS conducts tests of a portion of the system's controls. A third of the controls are selected for the first year after authorization, another third are selected in the second year, and all the controls are then tested again for the SA&A process in the third year. IRS refers to the annual testing process between authorization assessments as its enterprise continuous monitoring (eCM) program.

Although IRS has these processes in place, they were not always effective in determining whether policies, procedures, and controls were effective and operating as intended. Controls for the systems we reviewed had been recently tested and evaluated; however, some of the tests IRS performed were limited. For example, the most recent eCM tests for the administrative accounting system did not include tests of access controls, and other tests relied heavily on reviews of plans and policies rather than actual system tests, such as testing the system's configuration. In one case, testers concluded that encryption was in place by reviewing a diagram and interviewing key staff rather than performing system testing. Although such a methodology complies with NIST guidance for moderate risk systems, it does not provide comprehensive testing of controls for key financial and tax-related systems. Further, vulnerabilities we identified during our review were not known to IRS despite those systems being in compliance with the agency's policies on periodic control reviews and testing. We have previously made recommendations pertaining to the limited scope of tests, as well as issues related to IRS not clearly documenting and reviewing test results; at the time of our review, these recommendations had not been implemented. As a result, IRS has limited assurance that controls over its systems are being effectively implemented and maintained.

IRS also has processes in place to verify configuration management compliance; however, tools used in implementing these processes have shortcomings. In addition to tests and evaluations conducted on a yearly basis, IRS uses automated compliance verification tools to periodically test compliance with IRS's security policies for its three major computing environments—Windows, UNIX, and mainframe. IRS stated that these tools, among others, are used as an additional control designed to partially compensate for and mitigate previously identified risks associated with outdated software and missing patches for databases, as well as shortcomings in control testing of its mainframe system. However, the UNIX tool does not test whether appropriate security patches have been applied, and the mainframe tool only tests compliance with a limited subset of the agency's policies. Therefore, the results from these tools do not provide management with the information necessary to allow it to arrive at appropriate conclusions about the security status of these systems. As a result, IRS may not be fully aware of vulnerabilities that could adversely affect critical applications and data.

System Remedial Action Plans Were Complete, but Corrective Actions Were Not Effectively Validated

A remedial action plan is a key component of an agency's information security program. Such a plan assists agencies in identifying, assessing, prioritizing, and monitoring progress in correcting security weaknesses that are found in information systems. In its annual FISMA guidance to agencies, OMB requires agency remedial action plans, also known as plans of action and milestones, to include the resources necessary to correct identified weaknesses. According to the *Internal Revenue Manual*, the agency should document weaknesses found during security assessments, as well as planned, implemented, and evaluated remedial actions to correct any deficiencies. IRS policy further requires that IRS track the status of resolution of all weaknesses and verify that each weakness is corrected before closing it.

IRS had a process in place to evaluate and track remedial actions and had developed remedial action plans to address previously reported weaknesses, but it did not promptly correct known vulnerabilities, and its process was not always working as intended. For example, the agency indicated that 76 of the 105 previously reported weaknesses open at the end of our prior-year audit had not yet been corrected. In addition, it did not always validate that its actions to resolve known weaknesses were effectively implemented. More specifically, of the 29 weaknesses IRS indicated were corrected, we determined that 13 (about 45 percent) had not yet been fully addressed. For example, IRS stated that it had implemented a prior recommendation to improve the scope of testing and evaluating controls, but as noted in this report, limitations on the scope of testing continue to exist. This indicates that IRS has not implemented a revised process to verify that remedial actions are fully implemented, as we previously recommended. To its credit, IRS partially implemented 6 of these 13 recommendations, but did not implement corrective actions on all systems where the weaknesses had been identified. We previously recommended that IRS implement a revised remedial action verification process to ensure actions are fully implemented, but this weakness still persists. Without an effective process to verify that remedial actions are fully implemented, IRS cannot be assured that it has corrected vulnerabilities and, consequently, may unknowingly expose itself to additional risk.

Conclusions

Although IRS implemented numerous controls and procedures intended to protect key financial and tax-processing systems, control weaknesses continue to jeopardize the confidentiality, integrity, and availability of financial and sensitive taxpayer information. IRS made strides during the fiscal year in initiating efforts to address the internal control deficiencies that collectively constitute this material weakness. Notable among these efforts was the formation of cross-functional working groups tasked with the identification and remediation of specific at-risk control areas. In addition, the agency continued to make limited progress in correcting or mitigating previously reported weaknesses, implementing controls over key financial systems, and developing and documenting a framework for its comprehensive information security program. However, information security weaknesses existed in access and other information system controls over IRS's financial and tax-processing systems. The financial and taxpayer information on IRS systems will remain particularly vulnerable to internal threats until the agency (1) addresses weaknesses pertaining to identification and authentication, authorization, cryptography, audit and monitoring, physical security, and configuration management, and (2) fully implements key components of a comprehensive information security program that ensures risk assessments are conducted in the current operating environment; policies and procedures are appropriately specific and effectively implemented; security plans are written to reflect the current operating environment; processes intended to test, monitor, and evaluate internal controls are appropriately detecting vulnerabilities; processes intended to check configuration management are in place; and backup procedures are working effectively.

The new and unresolved deficiencies from previous audits, along with a lack of fully effective compensating and mitigating controls, impair IRS's ability to ensure that its financial and taxpayer information is secure from internal threats, reducing its assurance that its financial statements and other financial information are fairly presented or reliable and that sensitive IRS and taxpayer information is being sufficiently safeguarded from unauthorized disclosure and modification. These deficiencies are the basis of our determination that IRS had a material weakness in internal control over financial reporting related to information security in fiscal year 2011.

Recommendations for Executive Action

In addition to implementing our previous recommendations, we are recommending that the Commissioner of Internal Revenue take the following six actions to fully implement key components of the IRS comprehensive information security program:

- document a baseline configuration standard for tasks initiated on the mainframe operating system;

- document monitoring procedures that staff use to review audit logs for a key financial system;

- fully document monitoring procedures for the procurement system, specifically, supervisory review procedures to ensure access privileges are appropriate for segregation of duties;

- expand tests associated with the agency's enterprise continuous monitoring process to include tests of access controls and system tests, such as testing the system's configuration, where appropriate, to ensure comprehensive testing of key controls for financial and tax-related systems;

- implement a compliance verification application to ensure appropriate security patches have been applied in the UNIX environment; and

- implement a compliance verification application, or other appropriate process, to ensure configuration policies are comprehensively tested on the mainframe.

We are also making 23 detailed recommendations in a separate report with limited distribution. These recommendations consist of actions to be taken to correct specific information security weaknesses related to identification and authentication, authorization, audit and monitoring, physical security, configuration management, and contingency planning.

Agency Comments and Our Evaluation

In providing written comments (reprinted in app. II) on a draft of this report, the Commissioner of Internal Revenue stated that the security and privacy of taxpayer and financial information is of the utmost importance to the agency and that IRS will provide a detailed corrective action plan addressing each of our recommendations. Further, the Commissioner stated that the integrity of IRS's financial systems continues to be sound and that the agency has fully implemented a comprehensive information security program within the spirit and intent of NIST guidelines. However, as we noted in this report, although IRS has provided a comprehensive framework for its information security program, an underlying reason for the information security weaknesses in IRS's financial and tax-processing systems is that it has not yet fully implemented critical components of its comprehensive information security program. For example, although IRS had a process in place to evaluate and track remedial actions and had developed remedial action plans to address previously reported weaknesses, it did not always validate that its actions to resolve known weaknesses were effectively implemented. The effective implementation of our recommendations in this report and in our previous reports will assist IRS in protecting taxpayer and financial information.

This report contains recommendations to you. As you know, 31 U.S.C. § 720 requires the head of a federal agency to submit a written statement of the actions taken on our recommendations to the Senate Committee on Homeland Security and Governmental Affairs and to the House Committee on Oversight and Government Reform not later than 60 days from the date of the report and to the House and Senate Committees on Appropriations with the agency's first request for appropriations made more than 60 days after the date of this report. Because agency personnel serve as the primary source of information on the status of recommendations, we request that the agency also provide us with a copy of the agency's statement of action to serve as preliminary information on the status of open recommendations.

We are sending copies of this report to interested congressional committees, the Secretary of the Treasury, and the Treasury Inspector General for Tax Administration. The report also is available at no charge on the GAO website at http://www.gao.gov.

If you have any questions regarding this report, please contact Nancy R. Kingsbury at (202) 512-2700 or Gregory C. Wilshusen at (202) 512-6244. We can also be reached by e-mail at kingsburyn@gao.gov and wilshuseng@gao.gov. Contact points for our Offices of Congressional Relations and Public Affairs may be found on the last page of this report. Key contributors to this report are listed in appendix III.

Sincerely yours,

Nancy R. Kingsbury
Managing Director
Applied Research and Methods

Gregory C. Wilshusen
Director
Information Security Issues

Appendix I: Objective, Scope, and Methodology

The objective of our review was to determine whether controls over key financial and tax-processing systems were effective in protecting the confidentiality, integrity, and availability of financial and sensitive taxpayer information at the Internal Revenue Service (IRS). To do this, we examined IRS information security policies, plans, and procedures; tested controls over key financial applications; and interviewed key agency officials in order to (1) assess the effectiveness of corrective actions taken by IRS to address weaknesses we previously reported, (2) determine the extent to which compensating and mitigating controls presented by IRS address previously noted areas of concern, and (3) determine whether any additional weaknesses existed. This work was performed in connection with our audit of IRS's fiscal years 2011 and 2010 financial statements for the purpose of supporting our opinion on internal control over the preparation of those statements.

To determine whether controls over key financial and tax-processing systems were effective, we considered the results of our evaluation of IRS's actions to mitigate previously reported weaknesses, and evaluated a selection of controls that IRS asserted compensate for and mitigate known deficiencies. Additionally, we performed new audit work at the three enterprise computing centers located in Detroit, Michigan; Martinsburg, West Virginia; and Memphis, Tennessee, as well as IRS facilities in New Carrollton and Oxon Hill, Maryland; Beckley, West Virginia; and Washington, D.C. We concentrated our evaluation on threats emanating from sources internal to IRS's computer networks. Considering systems that directly or indirectly support the processing of material transactions that are reflected in the agency's financial statements, we focused our technical work on the general support systems that directly or indirectly support key financial and taxpayer information systems.

Our evaluation was based on our *Federal Information System Controls Audit Manual*, which contains guidance for reviewing information system controls that affect the confidentiality, integrity, and availability of computerized information; National Institute of Standards and Technology guidance; and IRS policies and procedures. We evaluated controls by

- testing the complexity, expiration, and policy for passwords on databases to determine if strong password management was enforced;

- testing the design of a key application to determine if the application's access controls are effective;

- reviewing access configurations on key systems and database configurations;

- reviewing access control/privileges for network folders to determine if system access is assigned based on least privilege;

- examining IRS's implementation of encryption to secure transmissions on its internal network;

- analyzing the effectiveness of IRS's monitoring processes for its systems;

- observing and analyzing physical access controls at each of the enterprise computing centers to determine if computer facilities and resources had been protected;

- examining the status of patching for selected databases and system components to ensure that patches are up to date;

- testing Domain Name Servers to determine if unnecessary services were running and if operating systems and software were current;

- testing servers to determine if extended stored procedures exist;

- evaluating the mainframe operating system controls that support the operation of databases related to revenue accounting;

- evaluating the controls of mainframe Started Tasks; and

- examining documentation to determine the extent to which IRS is performing comprehensive testing of its key network components.

Using the requirements in the Federal Information Security Management Act that establish elements for an effective agencywide information security program, we reviewed and evaluated IRS's implementation of its security program by

- analyzing IRS's process for reviewing risk assessments to determine whether the assessments are up to date, documented, and approved;

- reviewing IRS's policies, procedures, practices, and standards to determine whether its security management program is documented, approved, and up to date;

- reviewing IRS's system security plans for specified systems to determine the extent to which the plans were reviewed, and included information as required by Office of Management and Budget Circular A-130;

- verifying whether employees with security-related responsibilities had received specialized training within the year;

- analyzing documentation to determine if the effectiveness of security controls is periodically assessed;

- reviewing IRS's actions to correct weaknesses to determine if they had effectively mitigated or resolved the vulnerability or control deficiency;

- reviewing continuity-of-operations planning documentation for five systems to determine if such plans were appropriately documented and tested; and

- reviewing documented system recovery activities to determine if the system could be successfully recovered and reconstituted to its original state after a disruption or failure.

In addition, we discussed with management officials and key security representatives, such as those from IRS's Computer Security Incident Response Center and Office of Cybersecurity, as well as the three computing centers, whether information security controls were in place, adequately designed, and operating effectively.

We performed our audit from April 2011 to March 2012 in accordance with U.S. generally accepted government auditing standards. We believe our audit provides a reasonable basis for our opinions and other conclusions.

Appendix II: Comments from the Internal Revenue Service

DEPARTMENT OF THE TREASURY
INTERNAL REVENUE SERVICE
WASHINGTON, D.C. 20224

COMMISSIONER

March 7, 2012

Mr. Gregory C. Wilshusen
Director, Information Security Issues
U.S. Government Accountability Office
441 G Street, NW
Washington, DC 20548

Dear Mr. Wilshusen:

Thank you for the opportunity to comment on the draft report, *Information Security: IRS Needs to Further Enhance Internal Control Over Financial Reporting and Taxpayer Data* (GAO-12-393). We appreciate that your draft report recognizes the progress that the IRS has made to improve our information security program and that numerous initiatives are underway.

The security and privacy of all taxpayer and financial information is of utmost importance to us and the integrity of our financial systems continues to be sound. We are committed to securing our computer environment as we continually evaluate processes, promote user awareness and apply innovative ideas to increase compliance. The IRS has fully implemented a comprehensive information security program, within the spirit and intent of the National Institute of Standards and Technology guidelines.

We appreciate your continued support and guidance as we work to improve our security posture and look forward to working with you to develop appropriate measures. We will provide the detailed corrective action plan addressing each of the recommendations with our response to the final report.

If you have any questions, please contact me or a member of your staff may contact Terence V. Milholland, Chief Technology Officer, at (202) 622-6800.

Sincerely,

Douglas H. Shulman

Appendix III: GAO Contacts and Staff Acknowledgments

GAO Contacts	Nancy R. Kingsbury (202) 512-2700 or kingsburyn@gao.gov Gregory C. Wilshusen (202) 512-6244 or wilshuseng@gao.gov
Staff Acknowledgments	In addition to the individuals named above, David Hayes (assistant director), Jeffrey Knott (assistant director), Mark Canter, Sharhonda Deloach, Jennifer Franks, Mickie Gray, Nicole Jarvis, Linda Kochersberger, Lee McCracken, Kevin Metcalfe, Bradley Roach, Eugene Stevens, and Michael Stevens made key contributions to this report.

GAO's Mission	The Government Accountability Office, the audit, evaluation, and investigative arm of Congress, exists to support Congress in meeting its constitutional responsibilities and to help improve the performance and accountability of the federal government for the American people. GAO examines the use of public funds; evaluates federal programs and policies; and provides analyses, recommendations, and other assistance to help Congress make informed oversight, policy, and funding decisions. GAO's commitment to good government is reflected in its core values of accountability, integrity, and reliability.
Obtaining Copies of GAO Reports and Testimony	The fastest and easiest way to obtain copies of GAO documents at no cost is through GAO's website (www.gao.gov). Each weekday afternoon, GAO posts on its website newly released reports, testimony, and correspondence. To have GAO e-mail you a list of newly posted products, go to www.gao.gov and select "E-mail Updates."
Order by Phone	The price of each GAO publication reflects GAO's actual cost of production and distribution and depends on the number of pages in the publication and whether the publication is printed in color or black and white. Pricing and ordering information is posted on GAO's website, http://www.gao.gov/ordering.htm. Place orders by calling (202) 512-6000, toll free (866) 801-7077, or TDD (202) 512-2537. Orders may be paid for using American Express, Discover Card, MasterCard, Visa, check, or money order. Call for additional information.
Connect with GAO	Connect with GAO on Facebook, Flickr, Twitter, and YouTube. Subscribe to our RSS Feeds or E-mail Updates. Listen to our Podcasts. Visit GAO on the web at www.gao.gov.
To Report Fraud, Waste, and Abuse in Federal Programs	Contact: Website: www.gao.gov/fraudnet/fraudnet.htm E-mail: fraudnet@gao.gov Automated answering system: (800) 424-5454 or (202) 512-7470
Congressional Relations	Katherine Siggerud, Managing Director, siggerudk@gao.gov, (202) 512-4400, U.S. Government Accountability Office, 441 G Street NW, Room 7125, Washington, DC 20548
Public Affairs	Chuck Young, Managing Director, youngc1@gao.gov, (202) 512-4800 U.S. Government Accountability Office, 441 G Street NW, Room 7149 Washington, DC 20548

Please Print on Recycled Paper.